INTERESTING FACTS ABOUT VATICAN CITY

VATICAN CITY TRAVEL AND EDUCATIONAL FACTS BOOK FOR KIDS

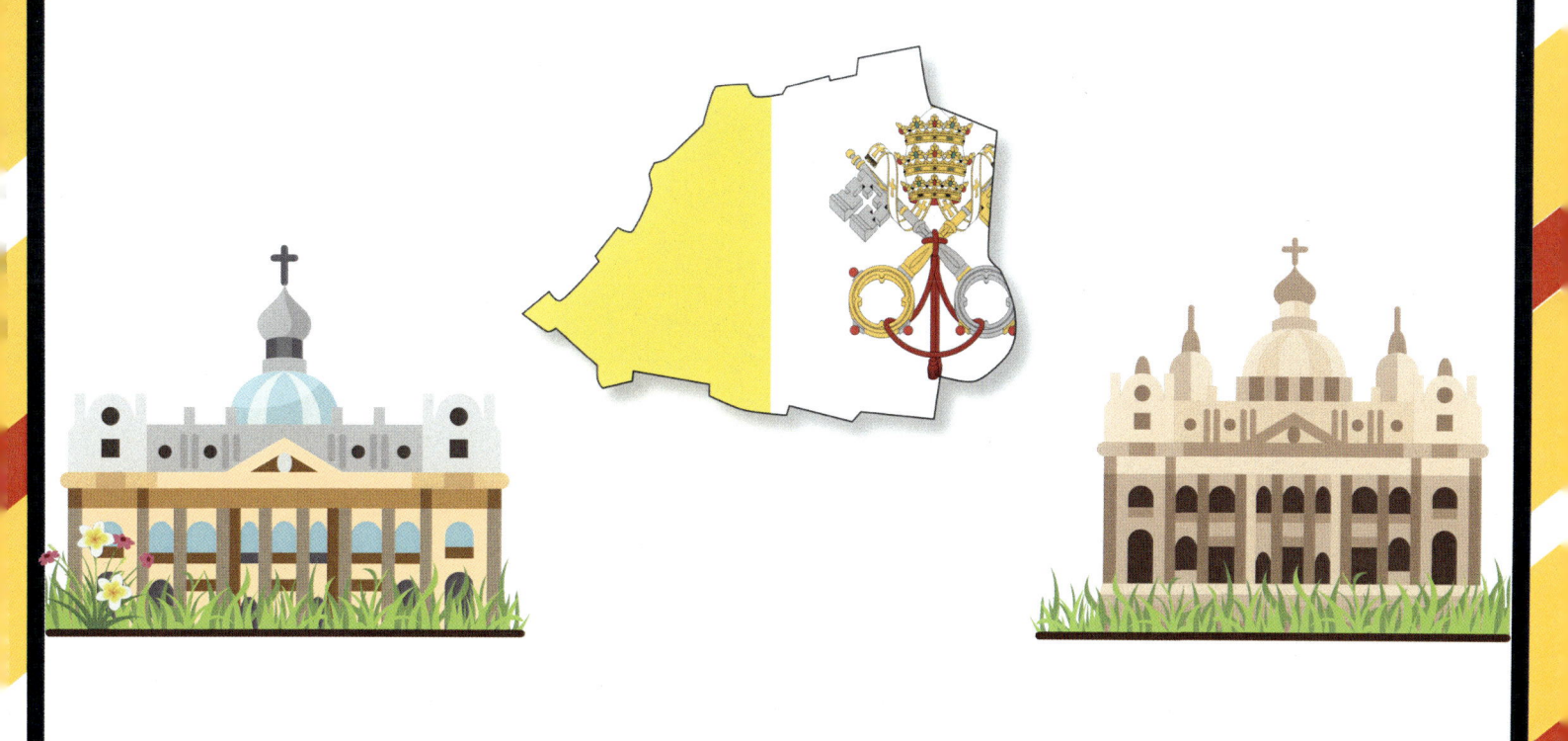

Copyright ©2024 James K. Mahi

All rights reserved

Vatican City is the smallest country in the world, covering only about 0.49 square kilometers (121 acres).

Which continent does Vatican City belong to?

Vatican City is located in Europe.

How many countries does Vatican City border?

Vatican City is entirely surrounded by Italy and does not border any other countries.

How big is the Vatican City?

Vatican City covers an area of approximately 44 hectares (121 acres).

What percentage of the world's land does the Vatican City occupy?

Vatican City occupies less than 0.01% of the world's land area.

What is the population of Vatican City?
The population of Vatican City is approximately 800 people.

Is the Vatican City overly populated?
No, Vatican City is one of the least populated sovereign states in the world.

What are the people of the Vatican City called?
People from Vatican City are often referred to as Vatican citizens or Vaticanese.

What is Vatican City's literacy rate?
The literacy rate in Vatican City is close to 100%.

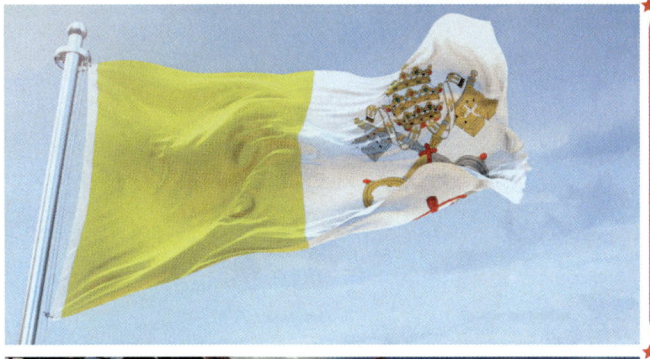

What is the official name of the Vatican City?
The official name of Vatican City is "Stato della Città del Vaticano" in Italian, which translates to "State of the Vatican City" in English.

What is Vatican City's nickname?
Vatican City is often referred to as "The Holy See" or simply "The Vatican."

Who ruled Vatican City first?
Vatican City has been ruled by the Pope, who is the spiritual leader of the Catholic Church, since its establishment as a sovereign state.

Which months are the coldest in the Vatican City?
The coldest months in Vatican City are usually January and February.

Which months are the hottest in the Vatican City?
The hottest months in Vatican City are typically July and August.

Since Vatican City is so small, you can walk around its entire border in about an hour.

It is an independent city-state completely surrounded by Rome, Italy.

Vatican City is the holy see of the Catholic Church and the home of the Pope.

The official languages of Vatican City are Italian and Latin.

Vatican City has its own flag, currency (the Vatican euro), and postal system.

The Swiss Guard is a special military force responsible for the security of the Pope and the Vatican City.

St. Peter's Square is a large public square in front of St. Peter's Basilica. It's a famous landmark.

St. Peter's Basilica is one of the largest and most important churches in the world. It is said to be built on the tomb of St. Peter, one of Jesus' apostles.

The Vatican Museums house a vast collection of art, artifacts, and historical treasures, including Michelangelo's Sistine Chapel ceiling.

The Vatican Library is one of the oldest libraries in the world, holding a massive collection of books, manuscripts, and other historical documents.

Castel Sant'Angelo is a massive cylindrical fortress now a museum.

The Vatican Gardens are beautiful gardens located within the Vatican City walls.

Vatican City has its own radio station, Vatican Radio, which broadcasts religious programming in many languages around the world.

Vatican City is a UNESCO World Heritage Site.

The official form of government in Vatican City is an absolute elective monarchy, with the Pope as the head of state.

The motto of Vatican City is "Non rec nobis, Domine, non nobis sed Nomini Tuo da Gloriam" which translates to "Not unto us, O Lord, not unto us, but unto thy name give glory".

The foundation stone of St. Peter's Basilica was laid in 1506.
The construction of St. Peter's Basilica took over 120 years to complete.

The Vatican Museums were founded in the 16th century by Pope Julius II.

The official currency of Vatican City is the euro, but it also mints its own euro coins with unique designs.

The national sport of Vatican City is association football (soccer).

Tiny Trains: Believe it or not, Vatican City has the shortest railway in the world! It's only used to transport goods, not people.

When you visit Vatican City, remember to dress modestly! This means your shoulders and knees should be covered when entering holy sites like St. Peter's Basilica.

The best time to visit Vatican City depends on what you prefer. Spring and fall offer pleasant weather, while summer can be hot and crowded.

The national symbol of Vatican City is the crossed keys of Saint Peter, which represent the keys to the Kingdom of Heaven, according to Christian tradition.

Hidden History: Underneath St. Peter's Basilica, there's an ancient cemetery where some important people from history are buried, including even some Popes!

Unlike most countries, Vatican City does not grant citizenship by birth. You can only become a Vatican citizen by working for the Holy See.

The highest point in Vatican City is the dome of St. Peter's Basilica.

One of the unusual things Vatican City imports is Swiss cheese for the Swiss Guards.

Vatican City has its own pharmacy and grocery store.

Vatican City issues its own passports, which are considered to be one of the rarest passports in the world.

There are no political parties in Vatican City.

Vatican City does not have an army.

The crime rate in Vatican City is very low.

The unemployment rate in Vatican City is 0%.

Vatican City does not compete in the Olympic Games.

The climate of Vatican City is Mediterranean, with warm, dry summers and mild, wet winters.

The internet domain for Vatican City is .va.

The time zone in Vatican City is Central European Time (CET) UTC+1.

The official residence of the Pope is the Apostolic Palace.

Vatican City has its own fire department and security force.

Collectively, the citizens of Vatican City are known as Vatican citizens.

There are no rivers or lakes in Vatican City.

There are very few cars in Vatican City.

The main mode of transportation within Vatican City is walking.

Since there is no airport in Vatican City, visitors typically fly into Rome's Fiumicino Airport.

USEFUL TRAVEL TIPS FOR VISITING VATICAN CITY:

1. **Plan ahead:** Vatican City is a popular destination, so it's wise to book tickets for attractions like St. Peter's Basilica and the Vatican Museums in advance to avoid long lines.
2. **Dress appropriately:** As Vatican City is a religious site, modest clothing is required. Avoid wearing shorts, sleeveless tops, or revealing clothing when visiting churches and other religious sites.
3. **Respectful behavior:** Remember that Vatican City is a place of worship for millions of people. Keep noise levels low, refrain from taking flash photography inside churches, and be mindful of others' religious practices.
4. **Comfortable shoes:** Vatican City involves a lot of walking, especially if you plan to explore the Vatican Museums and St. Peter's Basilica. Wear comfortable shoes to make your visit more enjoyable.
5. **Be prepared for security checks:** Security is tight at Vatican City entrances. Allow extra time for security checks, and avoid bringing large bags or backpacks to expedite the process.
6. **Follow tour guidelines:** If you're taking a guided tour, listen to your guide's instructions and stay with the group. Guides provide valuable insights into the history and significance of Vatican City's landmarks.
7. **Respect no-photography areas:** Some areas within Vatican City, such as the Sistine Chapel, prohibit photography. Respect these rules to preserve the integrity of the artwork and avoid disrupting others' experiences.
8. **Stay hydrated:** Carry water and take breaks, especially in hot weather.
9. **Explore more:** Besides the main spots, check out lesser-known places like the Vatican Gardens.
10. **Learn basic Italian:** Knowing simple Italian phrases can help in communication and show respect for the locals.

Thank You

Made in the USA
Monee, IL
08 April 2025